Irenaeus of Lyon

by Simonetta Carr

with Illustrations by Matt Abraxas

REFORMATION HERITAGE BOOKS

Grand Rapids, Michigan

Irenaeus of Lyon
© 2017 by Simonetta Carr

Cover artwork by Matt Abraxas

For additional artwork by Matt Abraxas, see pages 9, 13, 15, 21, 27, 35, 43, 47, 51, 53

All rights reserved. No part of this book may be used or reproduced in any manner whatsoever without written permission except in the case of brief quotations embodied in critical articles and reviews. Direct your requests to the publisher at the following address:

Reformation Heritage Books
2965 Leonard St. NE
Grand Rapids, MI 49525
616-977-0889 / Fax: 616-285-3246
e-mail: orders@heritagebooks.org
website: www.heritagebooks.org

Printed in the United States of America
17 18 19 20 21 22/10 9 8 7 6 5 4 3 2 1

Library of Congress Cataloging-in-Publication Data

Names: Carr, Simonetta, author.
Title: Irenaeus of Lyon / Simonetta Carr.
Description: Grand Rapids, Michigan : Reformation Heritage Books, 2017. |
   Series: Christian biographies for young readers
Identifiers: LCCN 2017039483 | ISBN 9781601784957 (hardcover : alk. paper)
Subjects: LCSH: Irenaeus, Saint, Bishop of Lyon—Juvenile literature. |
   Christian saints—France—Lyon—Biography—Juvenile literature.
Classification: LCC BR1720.I7 C37 2017 | DDC 270.1092 [B] —dc23 LC
   record available at https://lccn.loc.gov/2017039483

For additional Reformed literature, request a free book list from Reformation Heritage Books at the above address.

CHRISTIAN BIOGRAPHIES FOR YOUNG READERS

This series introduces children to important people in the Christian tradition. Parents and schoolteachers alike will welcome the excellent educational value it provides for students, while the quality of the publication and the artwork make each volume a keepsake for generations to come. Furthermore, the books in the series go beyond the simple story of someone's life by teaching young readers the historical and theological relevance of each character.

AVAILABLE VOLUMES OF THE SERIES

John Calvin
Augustine of Hippo
John Owen
Athanasius
Lady Jane Grey
Anselm of Canterbury
John Knox
Jonathan Edwards
Marie Durand
Martin Luther
Peter Martyr Vermigli
Irenaeus of Lyon

Table of Contents

Introduction 5

Chapter 1: A Student of the Scriptures 6

Chapter 2: In the Great Capital 10

Chapter 3: Pastor of a Suffering Church 25

Chapter 4: For the Love of Truth 32

Chapter 5: Protecting the Flock 42

Chapter 6: Peacemaker and Preacher 48

Time Line 55

Did You Know? 56

From Irenaeus's Pen 61

Acknowledgments 63

A map of the Roman Empire during Irenaeus's life. You may want to use it to follow his travels.

Introduction

Irenaeus was born around the year 130, about one hundred years after the death of Jesus Christ. After His resurrection, Jesus had commissioned twelve men to bring to all nations His good news of salvation, teaching them to obey His words and baptizing them in the name of the Father, Son, and Holy Spirit (see Matthew 28:18–20). These men included the eleven disciples who were left after Judas's betrayal and death, plus Paul from Tarsus, a former Jewish teacher and persecutor of Christians. The Bible calls them "apostles."

The apostles organized many churches and wrote letters to teach, encourage, and correct them when needed. Some of their letters are included in the New Testament. By the time Irenaeus was born, however, those twelve apostles had all died, and there were people who called themselves Christians but taught a different message. These people claimed it was a secret passed down by Jesus and His apostles to some "spiritual" people. It was often confusing. To help people understand the difference between the Bible and these other teachers, Irenaeus wrote a long book that is still useful today.

We don't have any images of Irenaeus from the time when he was alive. This is how nineteenth-century sculptor Carl Rohl Smith imagined him to be.

CHAPTER ONE
A Student of the Scriptures

Irenaeus was probably born in Smyrna (today's Izmir, Turkey). At the time of Irenaeus's birth, Smyrna had been part of the Roman Empire for over two hundred years, but Greek was still its main language. It was a large city of about two hundred thousand people, a busy seaport and an important stop for merchants and travelers from many parts of the world.

It was also a great center of studies, especially in the fields of science and medicine. Most likely, Irenaeus started school when he was seven, learning how to read, write, and do simple math. Normally, parents who could afford to give their children a good education hired tutors. Some families grouped their children together to share the cost of a tutor. School began at dawn, and discipline was strict.

This Roman mosaic shows a boy catching birds. Young Irenaeus might have worn similar clothes and played in a similar way.

At twelve years old, children began more serious studies, including the classic works of Greek and Roman authors. At sixteen, they studied rhetoric, which is the art of expressing well one's thoughts and opinions, and philosophy, the study of important questions about the meaning of life. Irenaeus probably followed the same course of studies. His letters and books show that he had a good knowledge of Greek poets and philosophers such as Homer and Plato.

He also learned to understand the Bible and the message of Jesus Christ. His teacher was Polycarp, who had been bishop (overseer) of the church of Smyrna for a long time. Polycarp had studied under the apostle John and had met other people who had been with Jesus. In his teachings, Polycarp repeated many things he had heard from them and explained how they were "in complete harmony with Scripture."

Ruins of the ancient marketplace at Izmir. We can imagine young Irenaeus walking by the stalls.

Polycarp thought it was important to stay faithful to the teachings of Jesus as they were passed on by His apostles. After all, if people call themselves Christians, which means "followers of Christ," they should follow His instructions and not something that other teachers made up. Sometimes Polycarp became so frustrated with these other teachers that he would cry, "O good God, for what times hast Thou reserved me, that I should endure these things?"

Irenaeus admired Polycarp. Like other students of his day, he probably took notes on a wax tablet, but because those tablets were meant to be erased and paper was expensive and could be ruined, he worked hard to commit Polycarp's lessons to memory. In his old age, he could still picture Polycarp sitting with his students or walking about. He could also repeat many of the things the teacher said and describe the place where they usually met.

We don't have any images of Polycarp from the time when he was alive. This is how nineteenth-century sculptor F. E. Ring imagined him to be.

Irenaeus worked hard to commit to memory Polycarp's lessons.

CHAPTER TWO
In the Great Capital

In the year 154, Polycarp went to Rome, the capital of the Roman Empire, to discuss some pressing issues with Anicetus, a bishop of that city. Irenaeus might have been in Rome already, or he might have traveled there as Polycarp's companion—probably on a merchant's ship like the apostle Paul used to do, because there were no passenger ships at that time.

Irenaeus traveled from Smyrna to Rome.
JEFF SLEMONS

Antoninus Pius

Rome was at the height of its power. The Roman Empire was the largest it had ever been, and Rome hosted over a million people born in different parts of the known world. The current emperor, Antoninus Pius, had been able to maintain peace within the empire, bringing security and prosperity to his subjects.

Christians were only a small minority of the population. Polycarp took the opportunity of being in Rome to pass on the teachings he had learned from the apostles. He was able to strengthen the Christians' faith in the Scriptures.

His meeting with Anicetus was also fruitful. The main point of discussion was the date of Easter. The churches in the East, where Polycarp lived, celebrated Easter on the fourteenth day of the Jewish month of Nisan (the Passover), no matter on what day of the week it fell. In Rome, it was always observed on a Sunday, because Jesus rose from the dead on that day.

In the end, Polycarp and Anicetus couldn't persuade each other but agreed to allow both practices so that the churches could be united. In the worship that followed the meeting, Anicetus allowed Polycarp to bless the bread and wine in the Lord's Supper as a sign of their unity in Christ. Irenaeus, who described the scene, was probably present, and that sample of unity and love left a lasting impression on him.

After the meeting, Polycarp returned to Smyrna while Irenaeus stayed in Rome, where he taught others as he continued to study. He also listened carefully to those who told a different story about Jesus and read their writings to understand what they were really saying. He especially spent some time talking to a group known as Valentinians, who met on the outskirts of Rome in one of the richest areas of the region.

The sample of unity and love between Polycarp and Anicetus left a lasting impression on Irenaeus.

IN THE GREAT CAPITAL

A portion of the Roman road called Via Latina, near Rome. Excavations along the same road (now inside Rome) discovered a Valentinian catacomb (cemetery).

The Valentinians believed they were more spiritual than other Christians and made it their mission to enlighten the others. They claimed to know secret things about God that were not written in the Scriptures, and they invited others to discover that "higher knowledge." Today, we call these types of teachers Gnostics, from a Greek word meaning "knowledge." Their message was tempting, because gaining higher knowledge seemed more exciting than admitting that human beings are limited and have to depend on God's written revelation.

Irenaeus listened carefully to those who taught a different gospel and read their writings so he could understand what they were really saying.

IN THE GREAT CAPITAL

Most likely, Irenaeus also met some followers of Marcion, a rich shipowner who at one time had been a great supporter of the church and later turned against its teachings. Marcion taught there are two different gods—a lesser god who was the creator (introduced in the Old Testament) and a higher god who was the savior (presented in the New Testament). Since the world has many problems and imperfections, he believed the creator could not be good; only the savior was.

Marcion believed these things so much that he wrote a book about them. He also created a new version of the New Testament, including only the gospel of Luke (starting at chapter 3) and some letters by Paul. In this version, he removed any mention of God creating and any references to the Old Testament. When he was finally expelled from the churches, he started his own.

Understanding these teachings allowed Irenaeus to talk more effectively to people who followed the teachings of the Gnostics and Marcion and to help Christians stay faithful to what the Bible actually says.

Irenaeus was still in Rome in 156 when the people of Smyrna joined in a violent persecution of Christians. In reality, the Roman government allowed its subjects to follow their own religions as long as they behaved and paid their taxes. Some foreign religions were even popular in Rome. The government just required an occasional sacrifice to the emperor as a sign of loyalty, and most people thought it was a reasonable request. Also, people who worshiped other gods didn't see any problem in paying respect to the gods of Rome as well. After all, they thought, it's good to have a lot of gods on your side.

That, however, was something Christians could not do. They believed there is only one God, who will have no other gods before Him. Because of their refusal to conform, they were often insulted and treated with suspicion.

The Pantheon was a temple built by the Emperor Adrian to celebrate "all gods," Roman and non-Roman. Egyptian gods were popular because Romans had a great respect for ancient customs and religions. Christianity, instead, looked like a strange, new religion.

IN THE GREAT CAPITAL

Besides, even though Christians dressed, spoke, and lived like most of the people around them, their worship was so different from the worship of the gods that many found it puzzling or even shocking. For example, when Christians talked about taking the body and blood of Christ in the Lord's Supper, people called them cannibals (eaters of human flesh). These things made Christians unpopular and put their lives in constant danger.

A Christian family, probably wealthy, depicted in the catacombs of Saint Gennaro, Naples, Italy. Catacombs were places where Christians buried their dead. In this picture a young girl, Nonnosa, stands between her mother, Ilaritas, and her father, Theotecnus. Their hands are raised in prayer, because that's how people prayed in those days.

Violence against Christians reached a frightening peak in Smyrna, with ferocious crowds bringing people to the authorities while shouting, "Away with the atheists!" They called Christians atheists (people who believe there is no god), because Christians didn't worship the gods of Rome.

At his friends' insistence, the elderly Polycarp hid in a farmhouse, but the local guards finally found him. At that point, he didn't resist arrest but gave his captors some food and asked them to allow him an hour in prayer. The hour turned to two. When he finally ended his prayer, they put him on a donkey and took him to the local Roman officer to be tried.

At first the officer attempted to convince Polycarp to offer sacrifices to the emperor. "What harm is there?" the officer asked. Polycarp refused. Next the officer asked him to join the crowd in shouting, "Down with the atheists!" The officer meant, of course, the Christians, but Polycarp shouted it while pointing at the angry crowd. Finally, the officer asked him to curse Christ. Polycarp replied with no hesitation, "Eighty-six years I have served Christ, and he never did me any wrong. How can I blaspheme my King who saved me?"

Normally, Christians who refused to worship the emperor were sent into the stadium to be devoured by wild beasts such as lions, tigers, bears, wolves, boars, and even crocodiles. In the Roman Empire, this form of execution was considered entertainment, and many people went to watch it. That day, however, the games in the stadium had ended, so the officer gave orders to burn Polycarp alive. Immediately, the watching crowd gathered wood for the fire. In most cases, the victims were nailed to a pole to keep them from running away, but Polycarp said that God would give him the strength to stay still and asked to be simply tied.

The news of Polycarp's death must have been painful for Irenaeus, who had a great love for his teacher. On the other hand, he knew that death for a Christian is not the end, because, as he wrote later, in Christ "the last enemy, death, is destroyed, which at the first had taken possession of man" (see 1 Corinthians 15:26).

Polycarp believed God would give him the strength to stand his trial.

IN THE GREAT CAPITAL

While he was in Rome, Irenaeus met other Christian teachers who were faithful to the Scriptures, such as the philosopher Justin (later known as Justin Martyr). In those days, philosophers were as popular as today's TV celebrities. They normally taught in public areas and lived together with some of their followers.

Philosophers valued reason and evidence and asked tough questions about popular beliefs. Justin, who had studied philosophy for most of his life, had become a Christian when he was in his thirties, about twenty years before Polycarp's visit to Rome. To him, Christianity was "the only safe and wholesome philosophy," grounded on more reason and evidence than other teachings.

Justin Martyr. We don't know exactly how he looked, but this is a modern artist's interpretation on an icon (a form of art typical of the Eastern Orthodox Church).

Neptune, the Roman god of the sea, as seen by a nineteenth-century artist, in Pont de Cité, France. Each of the Roman gods oversaw a different area of creation or of people's lives.

For example, the Roman gods and goddesses were all similar to human beings. They became angry at each other, and no one knew how they would react. In fact, sometimes their actions were so evil and corrupt that Justin thought they should be called demons. Instead, he introduced people to the one God of Christianity, who is perfect, unchanging, and without contradictions.

Besides, while there was no proof that the Roman gods existed, the God of the Christians had come to earth as Jesus Christ. His life, death, and resurrection had been predicted for centuries in accurate details and had later been confirmed by many eyewitnesses.

Justin devoted much of his time and energies to explaining all this to the people of Rome who had never heard about the Bible and God's promise of a Savior. He also wrote letters first to Antoninus Pius and then to the new emperor, Marcus Aurelius, explaining that Christians were not a danger to Rome, as some people thought. On the contrary, they were the emperor's "best helpers," because they loved order, goodness, and justice.

In spite of this, Justin and six other Christians were arrested and killed because of their faith. Irenaeus learned much from Justin, whether he met him in person or only read his writings.

Emperor Marcus Aurelius

CHAPTER THREE

Pastor of a Suffering Church

By 176, Irenaeus had moved to a prosperous region of east-central Gaul (now France) on the east bank of the Rhone River. A lively community of Christians, including Romans, Greeks, and Celts (or Gauls, as the Romans called them), had been worshiping in the main cities of Lyon and Vienne for a few years. Irenaeus might have become presbyter (elder) of Vienne soon after his arrival. In any case, he worked closely with the ninety-year-old bishop of Lyon, Pothinus. In those days, the words "presbyter" and "bishop" were often interchangeable, so we don't know if Irenaeus and Pothinus had different duties.

As the capital of Gaul, Lyon was an influential city and a lively center of trade. Every year it hosted a meeting of the sixty tribes of the area and a popular festival (called Festival of the Three

Ruins of the main Roman theater in Lyon, where the people sat to watch their games.

Gauls) that attracted people from faraway places. The festival included worship of the sun god Lugh (the Celtic version of Mercury, the Roman messenger of the gods) and worship of the emperor.

For about ten years, however, the people of Lyon had been troubled by serious problems. Germanic tribes had been repeatedly raiding the area, while a contagious disease (probably smallpox or measles) had been killing thousands of people. Many people believed their gods were taking revenge against the Christians, who refused to worship them. Because of this, they kept Christians out of public places and bullied them with insults. Irenaeus must have experienced the same mistreatment.

In the year 177, just before the main annual festival, the anger of the people of Lyon turned to extreme violence against those who were known to be Christians. In some cases, they attacked the Christians with rage, beating them, robbing them, and hitting them with stones. Then they dragged them to the public square to be judged by the local authorities. When the Christians admitted their faith in Christ, the authorities sent them to prison to wait to be tried by the governor.

An artist's conception of the emperor's defensive wars against the Germanic tribes that kept raiding Gaul

The local people kept Christians out of public places and bullied them with insults, throwing stones if they came near.

PASTOR OF A SUFFERING CHURCH

27

The abuses continued even when the Christians were finally taken to the governor. In fact, new people were arrested as soon as they were recognized as Christians. For example, a doctor was arrested just for making silent signals to those who were being questioned. A young lawyer was arrested when he tried to defend the accused. Even Bishop Pothinus was imprisoned and beaten cruelly, in spite of his age and poor health. He died in prison two days later.

Slaves received the worst treatment because, by Roman law, they could be freely tortured if they could give important information. Blandina, a young Christian slave, was tortured from morning to night. Her mistress was afraid the girl's frail body would not be able to stand it, but Blandina never renounced her faith. "I am a Christian," she kept repeating. "We have done nothing to be ashamed of."

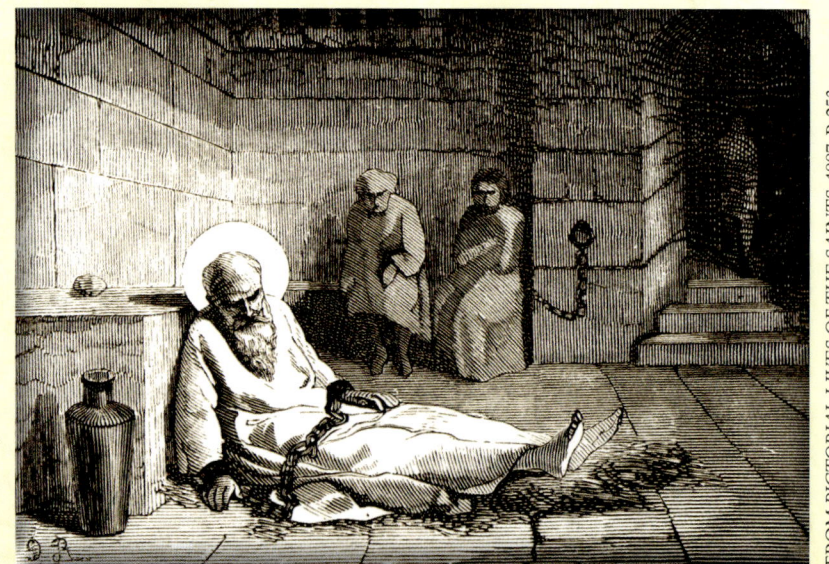

Pothinus in prison

FROM *PICTORIAL LIVES OF THE SAINTS*, 1887, P. 253

On the other hand, some slaves who were not Christians became more than willing to give false information in order to escape torture. They said Christians were eating human flesh and lived in immorality. Their reports made the crowd even more enraged against the Christians.

Eventually, the Christians were taken to the amphitheater to be killed by wild beasts. Blandina, who had become a favorite of the crowd, was hung on a pole, reminding Christians of the cross of Christ. When a fifteen-year-old boy, Ponticus, who had been brought to the amphitheater every day to see the other Christians tortured and devoured, lost any strength to resist,

Blandina

Blandina encouraged him and the other young people to stay strong. Finally, when the beasts refused to kill Blandina, she was placed in a cage with a raging bull that tossed her from side to side. By that time, she probably didn't feel anything anymore and died in the strength of her faith.

The authorities kept all the Christians who were Roman citizens in prison, waiting for the emperor's instructions. Marcus Aurelius replied that they could be released if they denied their faith in Christ. Otherwise, they were to be beheaded. Beheading was considered a "kinder" method of execution, reserved for Roman citizens. In all, forty-eight Christians were killed in Lyon.

Since Pothinus was dead, the church in Lyon needed a new bishop, and Irenaeus was their first choice. He had already shown himself a faithful and capable pastor. His church described him as "zealous for the covenant of Christ." Besides, his mild nature and personality matched the meaning of his birth name—"peacemaker."

In that difficult moment, Irenaeus had the responsibility of strengthening and encouraging the Christians who were alive and comforting those who had lost their loved ones.

Irenaeus had the difficult task of strengthening and encouraging the Christians who were alive and comforting those who had lost their loved ones

PASTOR OF A SUFFERING CHURCH

31

CHAPTER FOUR
For the Love of Truth

The citizens of Lyon were more triumphant than ever, praising their gods for the defeat of the Christians. They often made fun of them, asking, "Where is your God?" Those words must have pierced the Christians' hearts.

To Irenaeus, the greatest comfort comes from knowing God's loving plan of salvation for His children. The Bible teaches that evil and suffering came into the world when Adam and Eve, the first man and woman, rebelled against God, but evil doesn't have the last word. Through his disobedience, Adam has separated us from God, but Jesus, through His obedience, has reconciled us with God. That's why the Bible calls Jesus the "second Adam." Even if sin and suffering are still in the world, one day they will be gone forever. Irenaeus encouraged Christians to keep their minds on that final goal.

The disobedience of Adam and Eve has been redeemed by the obedience of Christ, the "new Adam" born of Mary.

Some people found it hard to believe. Like Marcion, they wondered how a good God could allow so much sin and suffering. Maybe there were two gods after all—the God of justice we find in the Old Testament and the God of love we find in the New. They wondered if the Scriptures were really God's only word, or if He had given some new revelation to some special people, as the Gnostics taught.

Knowing how carefully Irenaeus had studied these people's teachings, a friend asked him to write a book to help others understand what they really said and how they were different from the Bible. Irenaeus liked the idea. He wanted to help other Christians, and also the Gnostics, because, he said, he loved them "better than they seem to love themselves."

Roman writing tools

He wrote for many years, studying and researching both the Gnostics' writings and the Scriptures. In the end, he produced a series of five books. Today we call this collection *Against Heresies*. For Christians, a "heresy" is an opinion that is presented as biblical even if it goes against the main teachings of the Bible.

Sorting out the different Gnostic teachings must have

This sculpture at the ancient theater at Myra shows the masks that actors of Greek tragedies wore.

been difficult and tiring. To fill out the portions of the Bible that are mysteries to us (such as God's existence before the creation of the world), the Gnostics had created many complicated stories, talking about "pre-unintelligible pre-principles" and "spheres of beings"). Besides, their stories were all different from each other. For example, for some the "spheres of beings" were revealed through numbers and letters. Others gave them special names.

To Irenaeus, this was all so complicated that he had to end his explanation with the typical cries of Greek tragedies—"Iou, iou! Pheu pheu!" (which correspond roughly to our Eek! or Yeow!).

Irenaeus wrote for many years, studying and researching both the Gnostics' writings and the Scriptures.

FOR THE LOVE OF TRUTH

35

To prove the absurdity of these teachings, he used both humor and reason. For example, he imagined a "pre-principle, pre-unintelligible" royal being named Gourd (a type of squash) with a coexisting power called Supervacuity. The two emitted a fruit called Cucumber, with a coexisting power named Melon. After all, if the Gnostics came up with their stories, couldn't everyone else do the same? And why would one story be more valuable than another?

He also made fun of the Gnostic view that all liquids came from the tears of a female spirit, all solids from her sadness, and all light from her smile. Since tears are salty, Irenaeus said, how could they turn into rivers? Maybe her tears caused the seas and her sweat the rivers? He was joking because he wanted to show that these teachings made little sense.

To prove the absurdity of the Gnostics' teachings, Irenaeus imagined a royal story of Gourd, Cucumber, and Melon.

To Irenaeus, Marcion's teachings could also be disproved by reason. There couldn't be two contrasting gods, Irenaeus said, because that would make them imperfect or limited. Also, we can't call "god" someone who is evil or unjust or who makes mistakes.

Another argument from reason was the unity of the churches. While the Gnostics had many different theories, the Christian churches were all united in their main teachings, no matter where they were located—in Rome, in Gaul, in North Africa, in Asia Minor, and in other parts of the world. As a summary of the Bible, they all had a short statement called Rule of Faith (a shorter version of the Apostles' Creed), which was basically the same in every church and every language, even though the words changed slightly. This proved that their beliefs were based on the same teachings that Jesus passed on to the apostles, and the apostles to their followers. Irenaeus found them to be much more reliable than the new revelations of some people who lived almost two hundred years after Jesus.

The fish was one of the earliest symbols Christians used. Another symbol (on its left) was formed by placing the first two letters of the Greek word for "Christ" one over the other.

More importantly, why would Jesus teach something to the apostles and then reveal a different secret knowledge to others? And why would the apostle Paul go through all the trouble of starting and organizing churches and teaching them what to preach and what to do, only to reveal confidential truths to other people? To Irenaeus, it didn't make sense.

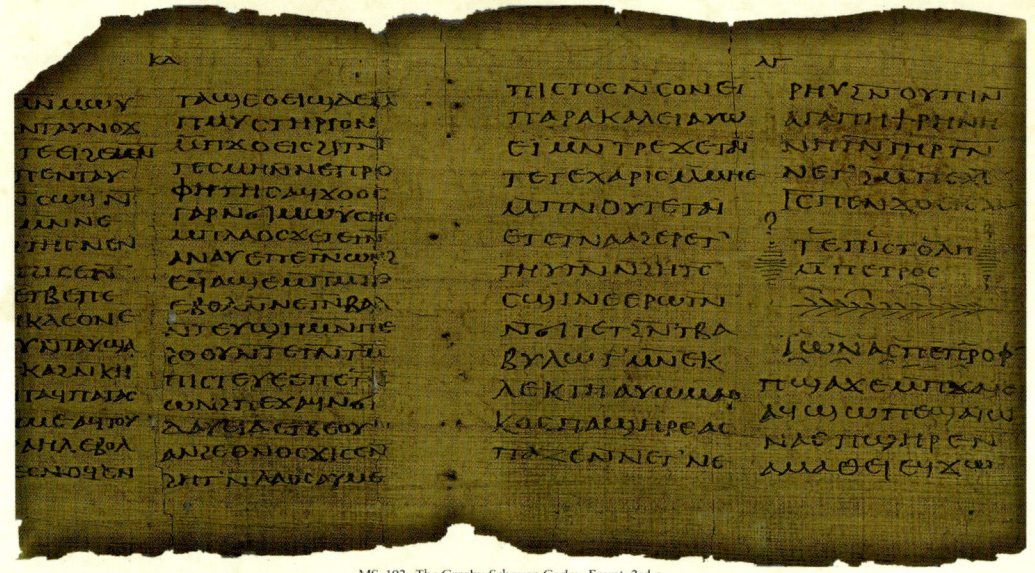

MS 193 The Crosby-Schøyen Codex. Egypt, 3rd c.
The oldest MS of Jonah and 1st Peter, and the oldest book in private ownership

Two pages from an ancient manuscript in the ancient Alexandrian library, showing the end of 1 Peter and the beginning of the book of Jonah. This is the earliest manuscript of 1 Peter in any language and the earliest complete manuscript of Jonah in any language. Manuscripts such as this were owned and recognized by Christian churches during Irenaeus's life.

Most of Irenaeus's arguments, however, were based on the Scriptures, which he quoted freely. God, Irenaeus said, has revealed Himself in the Bible, giving all the truth men and women need to know about Him and our relationship with Him. And the Bible teaches that there is only one God, in both the Old and the New Testament, and He is good, perfect, and just. In fact, from Genesis to Revelation we read one long, beautiful story: how God saved His sinful people.

Irenaeus used Bible verses, for example, to disprove the Gnostics' teachings that the things we can see, hear, and feel are just a weight that drags our souls down. The Bible shows instead that God's goodness is evident in everything He does and that the beauties of this world reveal His love, power, and wisdom.

To those who believed God is not interested in the things of this world, Irenaeus showed Bible verses that explain how He keeps it going day by day (Matthew 5:45), so that nothing happens by chance. In fact, God cares so much for this world that, Irenaeus argued, to reconcile sinners to Himself, He has taken a human body (John 1:14); lived a human life, eating and drinking real food; and died a real human death. Finally, because He rose, in body and soul, from the dead, Christians will also rise one day in new physical bodies (1 Corinthians 15:53; Philippians 3:21) and live with Him in a new heaven and a new earth (Revelation 21:1–2), which will be both beautiful and material (Matthew 26:27).

A starry sky. Irenaeus wondered if the critics of God's creation could produce anything better.

Irenaeus wondered if the people who criticized God's creation could ever produce anything better. "What heavens have they established?" he asked. "What earth have they founded? What stars have they called into existence? Or what lights of heaven have they caused to shine? Within what circles, moreover, have they confined them? Or, what rains, or frosts, or snows, each suited to the season, and to every special climate, have they brought upon the earth?"

If anyone needed help in understanding the Scriptures, Irenaeus encouraged them to go to the bishop of the local church—someone who was appointed by a recognized church and who could be trusted to interpret the Bible correctly, as the apostles had done before them.

If some verses were still a mystery, they should not look for "any other God besides Him who really exists." Instead, they should be humble and recognize that God is much bigger and wiser than any of them. He is the Creator, and human beings are only creatures.

Today, *Against Heresies* is still considered one of the most complete and accurate explanations from Irenaeus's time of the Gnostics' ideas. Besides, to answer the Gnostics' claims, Irenaeus had to study and explain the Scriptures in such depth that *Against Heresies* has become one of the first great summaries of Christian thought. We can thank the Gnostics for motivating him to write it.

CHAPTER FIVE
Protecting the Flock

Most Gnostics were not deliberately trying to deceive people. They sincerely believed that the Bible and the church didn't have enough answers, so they tried hard to provide them, even if they contradicted the Scriptures. Some, however, had selfish motives.

In the area where Irenaeus lived, for example, there was a group of Gnostics who attracted many people, especially women. They were followers of a man named Marcus. Apparently, Irenaeus was familiar with Marcus's tactics and with the accusations of some women who had escaped his charms. According to these women, Marcus used tricks with water and wine to amaze his viewers. Then he urged each woman to give a message from God. When they said they couldn't do it, he told them just to open their mouths and say the first thing that came into their minds.

An ancient Roman cup
LORD_KUERNYUS/ISTOCK

The Gnostic teacher Marcus urged women to give messages from God.

PROTECTING THE FLOCK

43

After the women had finally found the courage to speak, Marcus told them they had become prophetesses. This made them feel excited and thankful. Since most of them were rich, they showed their gratitude by giving him great presents.

Some of the women knew that the prophets in the Bible were always chosen by God. Those prophets knew that they could not just decide to prophesy when they wanted and never expected God to give them prophecies on command. The women realized that Marcus was teaching something contrary to the Scriptures, so they left him and reported some of his actions to their church elders.

Other women chose instead to stay with Marcus, even leaving their husbands to follow him. There were also some who were too ashamed to confess they had fallen for a lie, and they stopped going to church altogether. As he watched all this happen, Irenaeus felt distressed and alarmed.

According to Irenaeus, these fake magicians were the worst of the Gnostics, because they didn't even try to give a reason for their beliefs. They used their magic acts to attract people and to convince them that what they said was true. In reality, Irenaeus explained, their "miracles" never helped anyone. They never truly healed people or gave sight to the blind. They just wanted to amaze.

The Gnostics could be persuasive, because they used some words or sentences from the Scriptures to prove their point. In reality, they were taking these passages out of context to mean something different from what they originally intended to say. He gave the example of a poem made up of separate lines from different books by the Greek poet Homer. The lines had nothing to do with each other, but together they made up a poem Homer had never intended to write. A casual reader would think the poem was really Homer's. You can do the same with any poem or song. The Gnostics did that with the Bible.

Homer

Irenaeus told his readers it was important to examine every teaching and see if it agrees with the whole message of the Scriptures. He compared the Gnostics to the dog in one of Aesop's fables that let go of the good bone he had in his mouth to try to grab the reflection he saw in the water. He also compared their teachings to a beautiful object that seems more precious than an emerald, when in reality it is just glass.

To him, their teachings were also like a wild, ferocious beast that can hide well in the woods and can only be captured by bringing it out in the open. With his books, he wanted to bring the Gnostics' teachings in the open so that people could see them clearly and avoid their "assault."

"The Dog and Its Shadow," in *Aesop's Fables*, illustrated by Arthur Rackham, London, William Heineman, 1912

To Irenaeus, the Gnostics' teachings were like a wild, ferocious beast that can hide well in the woods.

PROTECTING THE FLOCK

47

CHAPTER SIX
Peacemaker and Preacher

As strongly as Irenaeus defended the unity of the church on biblical teachings, he was willing to allow for differences in less important things. In fact, he became particularly concerned when Victor, the new bishop of Rome, demanded that all churches in his city celebrate Easter on a Sunday.

It was the same issue Polycarp and Anicetus had discussed about thirty years earlier. Irenaeus was shocked to hear that Victor wanted to impose his opinion on every Christian, even though the Bible doesn't tell us when Easter should be celebrated.

Victor I, as envisioned by a later artist

Irenaeus was used to both customs. The church in Smyrna kept the Jewish calendar, and the church in Lyon followed the Roman rule. He didn't believe this issue was really important to the Christian faith. On the contrary, the fact that Christians could be united in spite of small differences confirmed their agreement in what really mattered. For this reason he wrote a letter to Victor explaining his thoughts. Other bishops agreed with Irenaeus. Finally, Victor agreed to allow both practices in the city, and the peace was kept.

Irenaeus wrote other books besides *Against Heresies*, but they are all lost, except for a copy of a handbook he wrote for new believers. In this book, he explained the unified story of salvation through Christ and listed the Old Testament passages about His coming—showing, once again, how the Old and the New Testaments are connected.

He also wrote many letters to guide and encourage other Christians and to discuss difficult situations. During that time, the Roman Empire was enjoying some political peace, which allowed both messengers and preachers to travel freely. According to some traditions, Irenaeus took advantage of this freedom to send missionaries to other parts of Gaul. In any case, his preaching and teaching prepared other men for this task.

In his writings, Irenaeus reminded Christians to be thankful for the order the Roman government had been able to maintain: "The world is at peace, and we walk on the highways without fear, and sail where we will." He believed that, in spite of their faults and corruption, rulers are appointed by God for "the benefit of nations…so that under the fear of human rule, men may not eat each other up like fishes."

A portion of the ancient road connecting Rome to France. This is one of the "highways" for which Irenaeus was very grateful.

According to some traditions, Irenaeus sent missionaries to other parts of Gaul.

PEACEMAKER AND PREACHER

This peace also allowed Irenaeus to preach and teach freely, so much that, according to a later historian, almost the whole city of Lyon became Christian. This might be an exaggeration. In any case, Christianity soon spread throughout the whole region of Gaul.

In spite of the temporary peace, however, he continued to encourage Christians to be ready to die for their faith. Even if there were no major persecutions in the empire, Christians were always in danger. Many of them, for example, were still mistreated and imprisoned, and some were forced to work in the mines in terrible conditions.

The first page of the oldest known copy of the gospel of John in Greek (Papyrus Bodmer II), from the late second century (when Irenaeus was in Lyon).

For some time, Irenaeus could teach freely in and around Lyon.

PEACEMAKER AND PREACHER

Irenaeus was right. In 202, while Septimius Severus was emperor of Rome, another widespread persecution raged against Christians. The persecution was especially fierce in Syria and Africa, but a later historian believes that Irenaeus was killed around this time. There is no proof of this, but since the last writing we have from Irenaeus is from the year 190, this date of his death might be fairly accurate.

Irenaeus is remembered for his work in helping the church to preserve the faith handed on by the apostles and to defend it when it was attacked. In *Against Heresies*, he taught Christians how to read the Scriptures faithfully and with humility, seeing both Old and New Testaments as one unified story. He also urged them to use their God-given reason to distinguish what he knew were historical events from imaginary stories. To Christians, these lessons are as important today as they were in his time.

Emperor Septimius Severus

Time Line of Irenaeus's Life

around 130 — Irenaeus is born.

154 — Polycarp (Irenaeus's teacher) goes to Rome. Irenaeus might have gone with him or might have been there already.

156 — Polycarp is killed by the Roman government.

177 — Irenaeus is in France, possibly pastoring the church of Vienne. The people of Lyon rise up against the Christians and imprison many of them. In all, forty-eight Christians are killed at this time. Irenaeus takes charge of the church in Lyon.

around 200 — Irenaeus dies.

Did You Know?

❦ In the Roman Empire of Irenaeus's day, young boys learned reading and writing from their parents or from a tutor. Girls learned whatever their parents wanted them to know—mostly how to care for a home. Boys continued to study as long as their families could afford it. Most of them went to work at a young age. In those days, sending children to work was not a crime.

This early education included penmanship and memorization. To practice their letters, children had wooden tablets on which the letters were engraved, so they could trace them over and over with their stylus (a pointed stick that was normally used to write on wax). These tablets trained the hand to draw each letter correctly. Writing was especially difficult for children who were left-handed or had poor eyesight, because everyone was required to use their right hand, and glasses had not yet been invented.

Memorization was also important. Some children were required to memorize whole books. There was no silent reading. People normally read out loud, or at least in a whisper. That's one reason why the Bible talks so much about hearing the Scriptures and not about reading them (Romans 10:17).

At about sixteen years of age, boys learned how to defend their ideas (rhetoric). Their exercises included defending a well-known character from the past, explaining the strengths and weaknesses of his position. Other times, they debated other students on a chosen topic.

- The Gnostics were in some ways influenced by the Greek philosopher Plato, who taught that the things we see are just an appearance of the reality that is beyond this world. He believed that only philosophers could understand the truth by thinking instead of looking around them. The Gnostics thought that only spiritual Christians could understand reality and despised the material world that we can see.

- Irenaeus was thankful for the Roman roads that led to every corner of the empire. In fact, the roadwork is one of the greatest achievements of Rome. The roads were built so well that many are still in use today.

    Initially, the Roman government built roads for military purposes to allow its troops to travel quickly and easily in all kinds of weather. They had to have a solid foundation, proper draining, and strong pavement. Sometimes they had to raise the road over the level of the ground, and sometimes they had to build tunnels through mountains. It was a difficult task, because they didn't have the instruments and the machines we have today. The same roads became important also to merchants and missionaries, allowing the spreading of both goods and the gospel.

- Even though there were efficient roads, the quickest and safest way to travel in the Roman Empire was still by water. To cross a sea, travelers usually went to the port and arranged a passage with a merchant ship. Then they had to stay in a nearby inn and wait for a messenger to go around shouting the news that the ship was leaving. They had to do this because ships didn't usually follow a schedule; the shipmaster waited for the right winds. There were also "unlucky" days when no one would travel or "unlucky" sights, words, and dreams that prevented a trip. For example, sneezing when boarding was a bad sign. So was the sight of a crow or magpie on the ship. Besides, travel by ship hardly ever occurred between October and May, when storms are frequent and the clouds too thick. It was done only in emergencies, such as a war or a famine.

River travel was also faster than road travel, especially if going downstream. Boats still carried goods upstream but had to be pulled from the shore by oxen or slaves using long ropes.

❧ When people met Justin Martyr, they could tell he was a philosopher just by the way he dressed. Like other philosophers, he wore a type of cloak called a *pallium*, grew a beard, and carried a staff. The *pallium* was a cloth worn around the body. It kept one arm completely free while the other rested on the cloth, almost like a sling. This type of clothing told other people that the person wearing it was worthy of respect. Other Christian teachers at that time wore similar clothes.

Under the *pallium*, the toga, or other types of outer garment, people wore a simple tunic, which was like a big T-shirt that went down to the knees. It was made with linen or wool. Common people and children wore only the tunic, especially in the summer. They kept the tunic on when they went to bed.

❧ Greek and Roman children played some of the same games we play today, like hide-and-seek and blindman's buff. They also played something similar to our game of marbles, but used dice or rounded nuts (like walnuts or hazelnuts) instead of small glass balls. Sometimes, they built small pyramids of nuts and took turns hitting them from a distance. They also pretended to ride horses, using sticks or canes.

Most toys were homemade. Girls had dolls, usually with moveable arms and legs. Some children even built their own toys. In the Greek play *The Clouds*, by Aristophanes, a proud father talks about his son who, "when he was just this tall…used to build houses, carve boats, make little wagons out of leather, and frogs out of pomegranate rinds."

❦ Roman government officials had an efficient postal system to carry their messages across the empire. They used messengers on horseback and had special places along the way where the messengers could eat, sleep, and change horses. These rest stops were equipped with stable boys, veterinarians, blacksmiths (to fix or replace horseshoes), and artisans who could repair broken wagons. They even had changes of clothes for weary travelers.

Common people had to find their own messengers. Most of the time, they sent their messages with friends who were traveling, because friends were usually more reliable than hired messengers. In an emergency, people could go to the port and ask some charitable traveler to deliver a message for them.

Letters were usually written on a sheet of papyrus, folded or rolled into a scroll, tied with a strong string, and sealed with wax. Official messages were sealed with a special seal that proved the message was authentic.

❦ Today, we don't have the complete writings of Irenaeus in the original Greek. We have a translation of *Against Heresies* in Latin and a translation of his handbook for new believers (*The Demonstration of the Apostolic Preaching*) in Armenian. Some researchers, however, have discovered in a city in Upper Egypt a small portion of *Against Heresies*, which was copied while Irenaeus was still alive. This shows how fast his writings spread around the Christian churches of his time.

❧ In one of his letters, Justin Martyr explained how they celebrated the Lord's Supper in Rome at that time. "And on the day called Sunday, all who live in cities or in the country gather together to one place, and the memoirs of the apostles or the writings of the prophets are read, as long as time permits; then, when the reader has ceased, the overseer verbally instructs, and exhorts to the imitation of these good things. Then we all rise together and pray, and, as we before said, when our prayer is ended, bread and wine and water are brought, and the overseer in like manner offers prayers and thanksgivings, according to his ability, and the people assent, saying Amen; and there is a distribution to each, and a participation of that over which thanks have been given, and to those who are absent a portion is sent by the deacons. And they who are well to do, and willing, give what each thinks fit; and what is collected is deposited with the overseer, who provides for the orphans and widows and those who, through sickness or any other cause, are in want, and those who are in bonds and the strangers sojourning among us, and in a word takes care of all who are in need. But Sunday is the day on which we all hold our common assembly, because it is the first day on which God, having wrought a change in the darkness and matter, made the world; and Jesus Christ our Saviour on the same day rose from the dead."

From Irenaeus's Pen

Irenaeus was the first theologian to talk about the Rule of Faith. The exact words of this rule changed from place to place and from church to church, but the contents were the same. Irenaeus thought this was a proof of the unity of the church.

In his *Against Heresies*, he includes a sample of this Rule:

The Church, though dispersed throughout the whole world, even to the ends of the earth, has received from the apostles and their disciples this faith:

[She believes] in one God, the Father Almighty, Maker of heaven, and earth, and the sea, and all things that are in them;
and in one Christ Jesus, the Son of God, who became incarnate for our salvation;
and in the Holy Spirit, who proclaimed through the prophets the dispensations of God, and the advents, and the birth from a virgin, and the passion, and the resurrection from the dead, and the ascension into heaven in the flesh of the beloved Christ Jesus, our Lord; and [who also proclaimed Christ's future] manifestation from heaven in the glory of the Father "to gather all things in one," and to raise up anew all flesh of the whole human race.

[He does so] in order that to Christ Jesus, our Lord, and God, and Savior, and King, according to the will of the invisible Father, "every knee should bow, of things in heaven, and things in earth, and things under the earth, and that every tongue should confess" to Him, and that He should execute just judgment towards all, [so] that He may send "spiritual

wickednesses," and the angels who transgressed and became apostates, together with the ungodly, and unrighteous, and wicked, and profane among men, into everlasting fire; but may, in the exercise of His grace, confer immortality on the righteous, and holy, and those who have kept His commandments, and have persevered in His love, some from the beginning, and others from their repentance, and may surround them with everlasting glory.

Here is a sample of a shorter version of the Rule written in Greek, probably around the third or fourth century, and discovered in Egypt in 1907.

> *Confesses the faith…*
> *I believe in God the Father almighty*
> *and in His only begotten Son,*
> *our Lord Jesus Christ,*
> *and in the Holy Spirit,*
> *and in the resurrection of the flesh,*
> *in the holy catholic Church.*
> —Dêr Balyzeh Papyrus

Acknowledgments

This was probably the hardest book I have ever written, because we know so little about Irenaeus's life. His theology is very important, but I had to work hard to ensure this book will be good for more than just putting my young readers to sleep. I thank God for giving me the strength to go on and for sending so many people to encourage and assist me.

I want to thank first of all my friend Daniel Coppin for insisting on the importance of Irenaeus for young readers, for reading my manuscript, and for making valuable suggestions. A huge thanks goes to Rev. Dr. John Behr, professor of patristics at Saint Vladimir's Orthodox Theological Seminary and author of *Irenaeus of Lyons: Identifying Christianity*, for his constant support, reassurance, and advice, and for reading my manuscript. I am grateful to both Dr. Michael Haykin, professor of church history and biblical spirituality at The Southern Baptist Theological Seminary, and Nate Milne, graduate from Westminster Seminary of California with a thesis on the covenant theology of Irenaeus, for reading my manuscript and making important recommendations. Heartfelt thanks also to Dr. Jeffrey Bingham, School of Theology at Southwestern Baptist Theological Seminary, who allowed me to call him and ask him a few questions about early Christian liturgy.

I couldn't have done without the encouragement of other friends, such as Elizabeth Nelson, Heather Chisholm-Chait, and Dianna Ippolito, who have read and critiqued my manuscript, nor without my usual cast of treasured young advisers—Lucy Plotner, Evan Olow, Israel Brindis De Salas, Iain Brown, and Isaiah Hasten, who listened to the reading of the manuscript and gave much-appreciated suggestions. What a surprise to see that they found the theological portions of this book the most thrilling and exciting! A special thanks also to Hannah Richard, my former Sunday school student, who has read the manuscript from her new home miles away from here.

Finally, but not less importantly, many thanks to my husband, Tom, to my kids, and to my church family, especially my pastor, Rev. Michael Brown, who was the first to introduce me to Irenaeus. My debt of gratitude to my publisher, Dr. Joel Beeke; director of publishing, Jay Collier; my editor, Annette Gysen; and all the staff at Reformation Heritage Books, who continue to exhibit unspeakable love and patience toward me. Besides making these books absolutely beautiful, they advise me and assist me with extraordinary wisdom and care.